I Love You To The Moon And Back Notebook
Lined Journal Gift Book
I Love You To The Moon And Back Gift Ideas
Paperback ISBN: 978-1-989733-17-2
 Cover Design by Sharon Purtill

www.ingramcontent.com/pod-product-compliance
Lightning Source LLC
Chambersburg PA
CBHW070515200726
48293CB00007B/2556

* 9 7 8 1 9 8 9 7 3 3 1 7 2 *